Loved

D1273204

E. M. Porter

ISBN 978-1-64191-590-8 (Paperback)
ISBN 978-1-64114-653-1 (Digital)

Christian Faith Publishing, Inc.
832 Park Avenue
Meadville, PA 16335
www.christianfaithpublishing.com

Printed in the United States of America

Introduction

As children, we were probably taught that praying is talking to God. But we may not have heard much about or thought much about God talking to us. I don't think I ever willfully set out to ignore what God was trying to say to me or tune Him out. I simply couldn't hear Him above all the noise as I went about living my life.

It's now when I am able to press the pause button, temporarily withdraw from the world, and shut out the surrounding din that I hear what the Lord is saying, understand what He's telling me, and experience what He's sharing. Consciously retreating to a place of both internal and external quiet has opened an ongoing conversation with the Lord.

The following emails and texts are the dialogue we've shared. Ever patient, God not only answered my questions but also quelled my fears and dispelled my concerns. And, above all, through these moments of stillness and quiet, He instilled in a me a deep awareness and confidence in both the simplicity and enormity of His love.

From: Me <me2@me.mail>
To: God <I.M.Yours@Love.God>
Sent: January 1, 4:55 p.m.
Subject: Hi

Dear God,

When I was growing up, I thought You were far, far away watching everybody and checking up on things. But all from a distance. I also thought that other than going to church and saying my prayers, I wasn't supposed to bother You too much. It was only a few years ago, well into my adult life, that I started to hear in homilies that You are available, approachable, and accessible—all the time.

I hope You're not angry that You didn't hear from me a lot apart from when I went to church or there was some sort of crisis going on. I thought this is how it was supposed to be.

From: God <I.M.Yours@Love.God>
To: Me <me2@me.mail>
Sent: January 1, 4:58 p.m.
Subject: Hi

Dear Precious Loved One,

Of course I'm not angry! I'm actually really glad you wrote to Me. I am also sorry that you didn't know that I've been waiting for you. I want everyone to know that I'm available any time, day or night. I am here for you all the time. And I love to hear from you.

I like when you tell Me what's going on in your life. I am delighted that you now know this. I am eager to be included in your life, and not just on Sundays.

From: Me <me2@me.mail>
To: God <I.M.Yours@Love.God>
Sent: January 1, 5:05 p.m.
Subject: Hi

Dear God,
    Does that mean that You want to hear about the boring day-to-day things or do You only want to hear about the big stuff?

From: God <I.M.Yours@Love.God>
To: Me <me2@me.mail>
Sent: January 1, 5:07 p.m.
Subject: Hi

Dear Precious Loved One,
    I like to know it all. In fact, I've been told I am very nosy. So go ahead and share everything! Tell Me about what makes you happy, what makes you feel angry or sad. I like to be the go-to person in your life. And there's no need to be concerned; I can keep a secret. Whatever you share, from the most mundane to the extraordinary, is just between us.

From: Me <me2@me.mail>
To: God <I.M.Yours@Love.God>
Sent: January 1, 5:45 p.m.
Subject: Hi

Dear God,
    That is really good to hear. It's great to have someone to share everything with. Are You sure You won't get bored though?

From: God <I.M.Yours@Love.God>
To: Me <me2@me.mail>
Sent: January 1, 5:47 p.m.
Subject: Hi

Dear Precious Loved One,
Don't worry, I never get bored hearing from people I love. And I love you nonstop; every second of every day. To put it in worldly terms, you could say I'm addicted to loving you!

From: Me <me2@me.mail>
To: God <I.M.Yours@Love.God>
Sent: January 3, 7:03 p.m.
Subject: Just Wondering

Dear God,
Since *I* thought I shouldn't bug You unless it's about something really, really important, I wonder if other people might feel the same way? Maybe some people think they should only go to You in an emergency.

From: God <I.M.Yours@Love.God>
To: Me <me2@me.mail>
Sent: January 3, 7:05 p.m.
Subject: Just Wondering

Dear Precious Loved One,
I'm afraid there may be a lot of people who think that way, but I wish they didn't. Of course, come to Me in an emergency, but I am not just like the trauma doctor in the emergency room! I can do a lot more than help out in emergencies.

Thursday, January 5, 8:21 a.m.

You must wish people knew that You're not just for emergencies.

8:22 a.m.

I certainly do.

8:23 a.m.

I really wish people knew I can take on any role they need. When you include Me in your day-to-day life, I see what you need and respond to those needs.

From: Me <me2@me.mail>
To: God <I.M.Yours@Love.God>
Sent: January 6, 12:15 p.m.
Subject: Quick Question

Dear God,

When people come to You, is there anything that makes You sad?

From: God <I.M.Yours@Love.God>
To: Me <me2@me.mail>
Sent: January 6, 12:20 p.m.
Subject: Quick Question

Dear Precious Loved One,
Well, I feel sad when I see people wounded and hurting; when they forget how wonderful they are. But when they come to Me, I can help them heal.

From: Me <me2@me.mail>
To: God <I.M.Yours@Love.God>
Sent: January 6, 3:42 p.m.
Subject: Quick Question

Dear God,
Is that what You mean when You talk about being like the ER doctor?

From: God <I.M.Yours@Love.God>
To: Me <me2@me.mail>
Sent: January 6, 3:43 p.m.
Subject: Quick Question

Dear Precious Loved One,
Well, not exactly. As a healer, I can transform your physical and emotional wounds from painful open sores to scars that no longer hurt.

From: Me <me2@me.mail>
To: God <I.M.Yours@Love.God>
Sent: January 9, 8:30 p.m.
Subject: Wounds, Scars, and Healing

Dear God,
 The other day, You mentioned that You transform our wounds to scars.
 But who wants scars? If You're really healing someone, why don't You erase the scars too?

From: God <I.M.Yours@Love.God>
To: Me <me2@me.mail>
Sent: January 9, 8:32 p.m.
Subject: Wounds, Scars, and Healing

Dear Precious Loved One,
 I am sure many people wish there was a magic eraser, but there isn't. Although no one really wants to have scars, with My Grace those scars lose their sting. Then they simply become reminders of where you've been.

From: Me <me2@me.mail>
To: God <I.M.Yours@Love.God>
Sent: January 12, 9:41 a.m.
Subject: Wounds, Scars, and Healing

Dear God,
 So even with traumatic experiences that have left deep wounds, You can help someone?

From: God <I.M.Yours@Love.God>
To: Me <me2@me.mail>
Sent: January 12, 9:44 a.m.
Subject: Wounds, Scars, and Healing

Dear Precious Loved One,
Absolutely! When you share your pain with Me, I can heal your deepest wounds. I don't erase the past, but I can help you be at peace with whatever or whoever has wounded you. And most importantly, I can help you see yourself as the beautiful child of God that you are.

From: Me <me2@me.mail>
To: God <I.M.Yours@Love.God>
Sent: January 12, 10:15 a.m.
Subject: Wounds, Scars, and Healing

Dear God,
So when You see us, You don't see all the scars we see?

From: God <I.M.Yours@Love.God>
To: Me <me2@me.mail>
Sent: January 12, 10:20 a.m.
Subject: Wounds, Scars, and Healing

Dear Precious Loved One,
Never. You're always perfect to Me. And when I have helped to heal a wound, you won't see those scars as painful or ugly reminders of the past. When you invite Me to help you, I can transform those scars so they become powerful, life-affirming reminders of how brave and courageous you've been in overcoming something.
Grace doesn't erase. Instead, My Grace is what enables you to be at peace with what can't be erased. In time, those scars can even become

something that causes you to smile and be proud of yourself. And love yourself even more.

From: Me <me2@me.mail>
To: God <I.M.Yours@Love.God>
Sent: January 12, 10:31 a.m.
Subject: Wounds, Scars, and Healing

Dear God,

I guess if You totally erased some of our traumatic experiences, we also wouldn't have the scars to remind us how much You helped us and reassure us about how much You love us.

Saturday, January 20, 1:31 p.m.

Can we talk about grace? It's a little hard for me to understand. Can You help me?

1:36 p.m.

Of course. Let's start with two very important things.

1:37 p.m.

It's available to everyone without measure and it's a gift from Me.

From: Me <me2@me.mail>
To: God <I.M.Yours@Love.God>
Sent: January 20, 10:02 p.m.
Subject: Grace

Dear God,
    I got Your text about grace and I understand what You said.

    But how and when do I get it?

From: God <I.M.Yours@Love.God>
To: Me <me2@me.mail>
Sent: January 20, 10:04 p.m.
Subject: Grace

Dear Precious Loved One,
    It's very simple. Just open your heart to Me.

    Maybe it'll be easier to grasp if I give you an example: Suppose someone has hurt you, in a significant way, and you're finding it hard to forgive that person. Even though you know in your heart it's best to forgive, sometimes the act of forgiveness can be extremely difficult. I completely understand that and am full of compassion when I see people struggle with this. That's why when someone comes to Me and wants to forgive and asks for My help, I always respond with an abundance of Grace. My Grace is what moves you to forgiveness.

From: Me <me2@me.mail>
To: God <I.M.Yours@Love.God>
Sent: January 21, 9:31 p.m.
Subject: Grace

Dear God,
    So is grace only related to forgiveness?

From: God <I.M.Yours@Love.God>
To: Me <me2@me.mail>
Sent: January 21, 9:32 p.m.
Subject: Grace

Dear Precious Loved One,
Not quite. Grace is universal. By that I mean it cannot be defined narrowly or confined to a list of specific situations or uses. It's not something that can be put in a box and wrapped up; it's not a tangible object that can be seen or touched. It's something that flows from Me to you and then emanates from within you—like joy.

Monday, January 22, 5:46 p.m.

So how do I know if and when I have received grace?

5:47 p.m.

You have probably experienced the gift of My Grace many times.

From: Me <me2@me.mail>
To: God <I.M.Yours@Love.God>
Sent: January 25, 8:16 a.m.
Subject: Grace

Dear God,
Can You give me an example of when I might have experienced Your Grace?

From: God <I.M.Yours@Love.God>
To: Me <me2@me.mail>
Sent: January 25, 8:18, a.m.
Subject: Grace

Dear Precious Loved One,
Well, when you're puzzled about something and ask for My help, Grace is what transforms you from uncertain to confident.
When you feel alone and abandoned, Grace is what invites you to trust in My abiding love for you and to fall into the safety of My embrace, even when you might not hear Me or feel My presence.
When the doors in your life seem to be closed, Grace is your silent companion who opens the windows and ushers in hope where despair had taken up residence.

From: Me <me2@me.mail>
To: God <I.M.Yours@Love.God>
Sent: January 25, 8:30 a.m.
Subject: Grace

Dear God,
So grace helps me when I'm stuck?

From: God <I.M.Yours@Love.God>
To: Me <me2@me.mail>
Sent: January 25, 8:33 a.m.
Subject: Grace

Dear Precious Loved One,
Yes, it definitely does that, but not just that. Think of Grace as the gift that inspires you to be your best self, in all situations and under all circumstances. Grace is what helps you to be more Christ-like, especially when you find that difficult.

From: Me <me2@me.mail>
To: God **<I.M.Yours@Love.God>**
Sent: January 25, 8:41 a.m.
Subject: Grace

Dear God,

Like when we're trying to forgive but are holding on to anger and resentment, or when we're afraid that forgiving will, in some way, diminish us?

From: God <I.M.Yours@Love.God>
To: Me **<me2@me.mail>**
Sent: January 25, 8:44 a.m.
Subject: Grace

Dear Precious Loved One,

Yes. It is My Grace that gently envelops you, guiding you to the path of forgiveness and helping you to open your heart and abandon your fears.

When you're mired in anger and resentment, Grace lifts you up and pulls you out of the quicksand of self-righteousness so you can move forward. With My Grace, you find that you're no longer paralyzed and suddenly you're able to stand tall and take a step forward. Like a divine escort, My Grace always shows you the way to joy and peace.

When you resist something and saying no is keeping you closed and away from joy, My Grace is what helps you get to "yes." And that "yes" opens your world and fills you with the promise of possibility. In these situations, My Grace enables you to find light where only darkness existed before.

From: Me **<me2@me.mail>**
To: God **<I.M.Yours@Love.God>**
Sent: January 26, 10:02 a.m.
Subject: Grace

Dear God,
    So grace is Your way of making what we humans think is impossible, possible.

From: God **<I.M.Yours@Love.God>**
To: Me **<me2@me.mail>**
Sent: January 26, 10:06 a.m.
Subject: Grace

Dear Precious Loved One,
    When you can't find a way and ask for My help and trust Me, that is often the case. That's when Grace becomes a divine translator that can help transform your incredulous questions and doubts into joyful songs of gratitude and peace.

From: Me **<me2@me.mail>**
To: God **<I.M.Yours@Love.God>**
Sent: January 27, 8:11 p.m.
Subject: Grace

Dear God,
    Is there anything that prevents someone from receiving or experiencing grace?

From: God <**I.M.Yours@Love.God**>
To: Me <**me2@me.mail**>
Sent: January 27, 8:13 p.m.
Subject: Grace

Dear Precious Loved One,
    The only thing I ask is that you come to Me with an open heart and trust Me. Without that, you're not fully open to the transformative effects of My Grace. There are things I can do for you, and with you, that are far beyond your capacity alone.

Thursday, February 1, 8:04 a.m.

Can we talk more about forgiveness?

8:07 a.m.

Of course. That's one of My favorite things to talk about.

8:08 a.m.

You could say I'm an expert on it. :-)

8:10 a.m.

That's great! I just have a few questions.

18

8:11 a.m.

What can
I help you
with?

8:14 a.m.

I think it may be
easier if I send You an
email. Is that okay?

8:15 a.m.

Yes, that's fine.
I will keep an
eye out for it.

From: Me **<me2@me.mail>**
To: God **<I.M.Yours@Love.God>**
Sent: February 1, 10:03 a.m.
Subject: Forgiveness

Dear God,

Well, we all learn that forgiveness is important and that we should always try to forgive people. For small things, it's pretty easy; but sometimes for bigger things, it can be really, really difficult. It may even feel like saying "I forgive you" is condoning something that's really wrong and very hurtful.

From: God <**I.M.Yours@Love.God**>
To: Me <**me2@me.mail**>
Sent: February 1, 10:06 a.m.
Subject: Forgiveness

Dear Precious Loved One,

Forgiving isn't the same as condoning or approving someone's actions. It's not saying that what the other person did was good or okay. It's saying that you don't want to hold on to anger and resentment, and that you bear no ill will toward that person. In choosing to forgive, you are handing it over to Me so you can heal.

If you don't forgive, you hold on to that wound. It stays with you and, over time, can fester. Forgiving is a big and important step toward healing that wound so it can stop hurting you over and over.

From: Me <**me2@me.mail**>
To: God <**I.M.Yours@Love.God**>
Sent: February 3, 1:42 p.m.
Subject: Forgiveness

Dear God,

So what do we do if we have suffered through a deep hurt or traumatic experience and we try and try, but can't seem to forgive? Or if we don't want to forgive because it feels like we're betraying ourselves and saying "It's okay that you hurt me."?

From: God <**I.M.Yours@Love.God**>
To: Me <**me2@me.mail**>
Sent: February 3, 1:45 p.m.
Subject: Forgiveness

Dear Precious Loved One,
*   I know sometimes it's not easy to forgive especially if you've been deeply wounded, physically or emotionally. If you or anyone else is having a hard time understanding the importance of forgiveness and how to get there, please come to Me.*
*   I am a great listener, so come and tell Me all about your experience and what is hurting you. Tell Me what's in your heart. Do you know how many times I've heard people say, "Lord, please help me. This hurts so much. I know You want me to forgive, but I can't. I need You. This is too big for me alone. I need Your help."?*

From: Me <**me2@me.mail**>
To: God <**I.M.Yours@Love.God**>
Sent: February 5, 7:32 a.m.
Subject: Forgiveness

Dear God,
    You mean all we have to do is ask for help? That's it?

From: God <**I.M.Yours@Love.God**>
To: Me <**me2@me.mail**>
Sent: February 5, 7:34 a.m.
Subject: Forgiveness

Dear Precious Loved One,
*   Yes. Come to Me with an open heart and I will always help you to forgive—every time, without exception. Just ask for My help and hand it over to Me. I will give you the Grace you need to forgive.*

From: Me <me2@me.mail>
To: God <I.M.Yours@Love.God>
Sent: February 5, 7:49 a.m.
Subject: Forgiveness

Dear God,
    No offense, but it sounds too easy.

From: God <I.M.Yours@Love.God>
To: Me <me2@me.mail>
Sent: February 5, 7:53 a.m.
Subject: Forgiveness

Dear Precious Loved One,
    For some people, it probably is very easy. But others have a hard time truly handing it over to Me and leaving it with Me. Letting Me handle it in My way and according to My schedule requires trusting Me fully and giving up control.
    I've noticed that people don't always like to give up control. They work hard to have control at their jobs, in their families, and even with friends. So I try to be patient and show people that I love them and encourage them to trust Me.

From: Me <me2@me.mail>
To: God <I.M.Yours@Love.God>
Sent: February 7, 5:21 p.m.
Subject: Trust

Dear God,
    Do You get angry when people don't trust You?

From: God <I.M.Yours@Love.God>
To: Me <me2@me.mail>
Sent: February 7, 5:24 p.m.
Subject: Trust

Dear Precious Loved One,
I don't get angry. I realize that many, many people like to be in charge and do things their *way, according to* their *plans and based on* their *schedule.*
At times I do feel sad when I watch people struggle because I know they don't have to. But sometimes people need to learn by having experiences; that's human nature. If and when they realize their way isn't working, I am here to help them and I greet them with open arms. (And I never say "I told you so" :-).)

From: Me <me2@me.mail>
To: God <I.M.Yours@Love.God>
Sent: February 8, 10:13 a.m.
Subject: Trust

Dear God,
Do You think people can learn to trust You?

From: God <I.M.Yours@Love.God>
To: Me <me2@me.mail>
Sent: February 8, 10:15 a.m.
Subject: Trust

Dear Precious Loved One,
Absolutely! That's one of My favorite things—when I see people grow in their love and trust of Me. It's beautiful to watch because I can see them change as they realize their load becomes lighter and lighter as they trust Me more and more.

When people really trust Me, they are happier and more joyful. They don't worry about every little thing, or even all of the big things because they know I'm helping them (and sometimes in ways they may not even realize).

From: Me <me2@me.mail>
To: God <I.M.Yours@Love.God>
Sent: February 8, 9:21 p.m.
Subject: Trust

Dear God,

So how do we do that—learn to trust? For example, let's say I have a hard time handing things over to You and really trusting You implicitly, how can I change that?

From: God <I.M.Yours@Love.God>
To: Me <me2@me.mail>
Sent: February 8, 9:25 p.m.
Subject: Trust

Dear Precious Loved One,

Well the first thing is to be willing to try. I absolutely love when people try, especially when they're a little apprehensive. I really think it just takes practice. Trust Me with something small. When you see that it works out well, you do it again, and again.

Then when you feel ready (or maybe even when you're not quite ready :-)!), trust Me with something bigger. As you keep doing this, it will become easier and easier. You'll experience My love and see how I take care of you over and over. Your trust and confidence will grow and grow, and pretty soon you won't even think about it. Over time, trusting Me and handing things over to Me with total confidence will come to you naturally.

From: Me <me2@me.mail>
To: God <I.M.Yours@Love.God>
Sent: February 11, 8:37 a.m.
Subject: Trust

Dear God,
   Is trust the most important thing in a relationship with You? It seems that without trust the relationship is kind of limited.

From: God <I.M.Yours@Love.God>
To: Me <me2@me.mail>
Sent: February 11, 8:39 a.m.
Subject: Trust

Dear Precious Loved One,
   In many ways, a relationship with Me is like other relationships you have with friends and family. The more honest and open we are, the more we trust each other, and the more we reveal about ourselves to one another, the more intimate our relationship can be.

From: Me <me2@me.mail>
To: God <I.M.Yours@Love.God>
Sent: February 12, 9:16 a.m.
Subject: Having a Relationship

Dear God,
   So if someone wants to have a relationship with You—I mean a real relationship with You, beyond going to church and saying the Our Father—what do we do? In some ways, I think it's a little intimidating to just say "Okay, I want to have a relationship with God."
   Where do we start? I don't know what to do and part of me worries that You have a lot to do or emergencies to care of, and You must have bigger more important things going on.

From: God <I.M.Yours@Love.God>
To: Me <me2@me.mail>
Sent: February 12, 9:18 a.m.
Subject: Having a Relationship

Dear Precious Loved One,

If that is what's keeping you, or anyone else, from having what you call a "real" relationship with Me, then I am very relieved and you should be too! You see, I'm never, ever, ever too busy to spend time with you or anyone else. I'm always interested in what you have to say and you always have My undivided attention. And no need to worry, there's no right or wrong way to have a relationship with Me.

From: Me <me2@me.mail>
To: God <I.M.Yours@Love.God>
Sent: February 12, 10:06 a.m.
Subject: Having a Relationship

Dear God,

You actually make it sound a lot less intimidating than I thought. But are there any dos and don'ts? (I guess there's no book to read like "Having a Relationship with God For Dummies.")

From: God <I.M.Yours@Love.God>
To: Me <me2@me.mail>
Sent: February 12, 10:09 a.m.
Subject: Having a Relationship

Dear Precious Loved One,

There aren't any set parameters or a how-to manual to follow. All you need to know is that I love you beyond what you can possibly imagine; I will never stop loving you; and more than anything, I want to hear from you and spend time with you.

If you really want a requirement, here it is: Share yourself. The only "must" is to share yourself with Me.

Tuesday, February 13, 5:03 p.m.

So all it takes to have a relationship with You is to share?

5:04 p.m.

Yes, it's that simple.

5:07 p.m.

Wow. I guess I'm not used to thinking about things related to religion as being so simple and easy.

5:08 p.m.

I realize a lot of people— maybe even you—might be accustomed to rules when it comes to religion, but spending time with Me is definitely not about rules. When you have a relationship with Me, I don't want you to worry about doing it right or wrong. There is no such thing.

So for people used to rules, there are no "Ten Commandments for Having a Relationship with God"?

5:10 p.m.

5:11 p.m.

Ha, ha. Just kidding :-)

5:12 p.m.

No, there definitely is not a list of commandments. As I mentioned before, sharing yourself is the most important thing.

5:15 p.m.

Okay.

5:17 p.m.

The more you share, trust, and reveal yourself to Me, the more you'll feel My presence in your life.

From: Me <me2@me.mail>
To: God <I.M.Yours@Love.God>
Sent: February 15, 12:04 p.m.
Subject: Sharing

Dear God,
Does it matter *when* we share with You?

From: God <I.M.Yours@Love.God>
To: Me <me2@me.mail>
Sent: February 15, 12:07 p.m.
Subject: Sharing

Dear Precious Loved One,
Definitely not. You can share whenever you want.

You don't need an appointment. You can spend time with Me whenever you choose—in the morning, right before bed, in the middle of the night when you can't sleep. Anytime is fine. You have My attention 24/7.

From: Me <me2@me.mail>
To: God <I.M.Yours@Love.God>
Sent: February 15, 12:30 p.m.
Subject: Sharing

Dear God,
Do You care *where* we are when we share?

From: God <I.M.Yours@Love.God>
To: Me <me2@me.mail>
Sent: February 15, 12:32 p.m.
Subject: Sharing

Dear Precious Loved One,
  No, it doesn't matter where you share.

  I realize people have busy, sometimes hectic lives, so feel free to share yourself with Me anywhere you want—at home, on the way to work, in church, in the car, on the train or plane, on a park bench. I am not a God restricted by location; you pick the place and I'll be there. Think of Me as your own personal WiFi hotspot. I'm with you no matter where you are.

From: Me <me2@me.mail>
To: God <I.M.Yours@Love.God>
Sent: February 15, 1:02 p.m.
Subject: Sharing

Dear God,
  Does it matter *how* we share? Is there a special way to share?

From: God <I.M.Yours@Love.God>
To: Me <me2@me.mail>
Sent: February 15, 1:04 p.m.
Subject: Sharing

Dear Precious Loved One,
  Absolutely not. How you share is as unique as who you are. Just be yourself and do what comes naturally.
  Maybe you want to start with something familiar—a prayer you know and like. Or perhaps you want to learn new prayers and make them your own; something special that we share. Another way to share

yourself with Me is to talk to Me like a friend. Tell Me what's going on in your world. You don't always have to do all the talking; you can also sit quietly and listen to Me. How you share doesn't always have to be the same; it may change from day to day. The only real requirement is to share with an open heart.

From: Me **<me2@me.mail>**
To: God **<I.M.Yours@Love.God>**
Sent: February 15, 1:32 p.m.
Subject: Sharing

Dear God,
    I think I already know the answer to this one, but I'll ask it anyway. Can we share anything we want? Do You care *what* we share?

From: God **<I.M.Yours@Love.God>**
To: Me **<me2@me.mail>**
Sent: February 15, 1:34 p.m.
Subject: Sharing

Dear Precious Loved One,
    Please, go ahead and share whatever you want. There are absolutely no restrictions.
    When you set aside time with Me, nothing is too big or too small to share. I want to know about anything and everything. Tell Me what you're happy about, worried about, what's happening with your family, what's going on at work, what keeps you awake at night, what makes you jump up and down for joy and say "yippee." Like I said before, I am nosy—really nosy. So you can feel completely free to share it all. There's no need to censor what you tell Me.

31

From: Me <me2@me.mail>
To: God <I.M.Yours@Love.God>
Sent: February 15, 2:31 p.m.
Subject: Sharing

Dear God,
Do You care *why* we share?

From: God <I.M.Yours@Love.God>
To: Me <me2@me.mail>
Sent: February 15, 2:34 p.m.
Subject: Sharing

Dear Precious Loved One,
No, it definitely doesn't matter why you share.
I'm sure you know people who only seem to come around when the chips are down and they need a shoulder to cry on. And even though you want to be supportive and compassionate, you might find this a little tiresome. Well that's one way in which we're different. A lot of people come to Me when there are problems. That's human nature. I have really, really big shoulders and I'm happy to let anyone—you included—cry on them, time and time again.
I understand the world you live in isn't always easy. So don't think that coming to Me because you're sad, angry, or hurt is a bad thing. That's why I am here! I don't get tired of hearing about your trials and tribulations. I like when you share them because I know I can help you.
Did you know that part of My job description is to help you, and others, learn and grow through difficult experiences? That's one of the ways I get to show you how much I love you. So please come to Me. I love you and look forward to any chance you give Me to help you. By the way, of course, I like to hear about the good things, so don't forget to share them too. It's nice when you give Me something to smile about.

From: Me <me2@me.mail>
To: God <I.M.Yours@Love.God>
Sent: February 17, 8:23 a.m.
Subject: Sharing

Dear God,
   Well, it sounds like there's nothing stopping anyone from having a relationship with You. From what You described, the time, place, method, content, and reason don't matter—anything we choose is fine.

From: God <I.M.Yours@Love.God>
To: Me <me2@me.mail>
Sent: February 17, 8:25 a.m.
Subject: Sharing

Dear Precious Loved One,
   That's it! Exactly!!

   Like I said, the only thing that does matter is that you share yourself—through whatever means you choose. Whatever works for you, works for Me. Anything is perfect. And, remember, the more you share, the more you will be aware of My presence in your life. Then you can begin to understand how much I delight in you and how much I want you to be happy and filled with joy. And most importantly, you can experience My love for you.

From: Me <me2@me.mail>
To: God <I.M.Yours@Love.God>
Sent: February 20, 5:48 p.m.
Subject: Love

Dear God,
   One thing that I've heard a lot is that there's nothing we can do to earn Your love; that Your love is not based on merit; and that You just love us all the time. Period.

From: God <I.M.Yours@Love.God>
To: Me <me2@me.mail>
Sent: February 20, 5:51 p.m.
Subject: Love

Dear Precious Loved One,
That is absolutely true. You get 100% of My love all the time and there is nothing you can do to deserve it or stop it.

From: Me <me2@me.mail>
To: God <I.M.Yours@Love.God>
Sent: February 22, 2:13 p.m.
Subject: Love

Dear God,
It's a little hard to fathom that no matter what we do, You love us. In our day-to-day lives and in our interactions with people, I think we sometimes, consciously or unconsciously, like to check and see if we're getting what we think we've earned, or if we're being treated fairly, or even if we're being loved the way we feel we should be loved.

It seems like the world we live in puts so much emphasis on achievement and entitlement that we bring that way of thinking into our relationships, and we like to be able to evaluate how we're doing and if we're getting what we think we deserve.

From: God <I.M.Yours@Love.God>
To: Me <me2@me.mail>
Sent: February 22, 2:17 p.m.
Subject: Love

Dear Precious Loved One,
Well as you've probably guessed, it doesn't work that way with Me. Try not to think of a relationship with Me in the context of what is very

often a quid pro quo *world. With Me, there is no scorecard. I don't meticulously keep track of what you're up to and don't ever dole out My love based on merit.*

From: Me <me2@me.mail>
To: God <I.M.Yours@Love.God>
Sent: February 23, 8:22 a.m.
Subject: Love

Dear God,

I guess we're probably used to viewing ourselves and our relationships in terms of what we need to do to *earn* or *deserve* something like someone's love, someone's friendship, a promotion.

As You said, maybe sometimes we live our lives with a *quid pro quo* mentality, so the idea of a relationship without even a hint of "if this, then that" is a little unusual or uncomfortable to us. Without some sort of built-in scorecard, I guess we're afraid the relationship runs the risk of becoming one-sided, which defies our desire for equality or balance.

From: God <I.M.Yours@Love.God>
To: Me <me2@me.mail>
Sent: February 23, 8:26 a.m.
Subject: Love

Dear Precious Loved One,

It's probably not surprising to you that I don't care about balance, not even a little. I can't. I love you too much. When it comes to My love for you, I have no sense of proportion.

I don't want to spend My time deciding who deserves My love and who doesn't, or how much someone deserves. You, and everyone else, get it all, all the time.

From: Me <me2@me.mail>
To: God <I.M.Yours@Love.God>
Sent: February 23, 3:02 p.m.
Subject: Love

Dear God,

    So in our relationship with You, we really just need to let go of our inherent human yearning for what we think of as relationship fairness. From what You've said, it sounds like it's never fair.

From: God <I.M.Yours@Love.God>
To: Me <me2@me.mail>
Sent: February 23, 3:07 p.m.
Subject: Love

Dear Precious Loved One,

    That's true. Fairness has nothing to do with My relationships. They are never fair and there is no balance. As the saying goes, the scales are tipped in your favor. They always are. You get 100% of My love. Period.

From: Me <me2@me.mail>
To: God <I.M.Yours@Love.God>
Sent: February 25, 9:21 a.m.
Subject: Love

Dear God,

    So what are we supposed to do in our relationship with You when it's based on such blatant inequality? It's so different from how we function in the rest of our lives.

From: God <I.M.Yours@Love.God>
To: Me <me2@me.mail>
Sent: February 25, 9:25 a.m.
Subject: Love

Dear Precious Loved One,
There is just one thing that I ask you to do in your relationship with
Me: Be your true self.

In other relationships, I often see people spend their time and
energy angling to get praise and aspiring to be the best son, daughter,
brother, sister, husband, wife, mother, father, friend, neighbor, volun-
teer, employee. But if you spend your time only living up to others' expec-
tations and trying to be the best in someone else's eyes, over time you may
end up masking your true self, or parts of it. For example, you might try
to conceal your fears, disguise your frailties, or deny your mistakes. By
doing this, you could end up losing your sense of self and forgetting who
the real you is.

You don't ever need to do that with Me. Just be yourself. To Me,
being the best simply means being yourself—whatever that is, at that
moment.

From: Me <me2@me.mail>
To: God <I.M.Yours@Love.God>
Sent: February 25, 4:11 p.m.
Subject: Love

Dear God,
Does that mean that with You it's always a come-as-you-are
party?

From: God <**I.M.Yours@Love.God**>
To: Me <**me2@me.mail**>
Sent: February 25, 4:14 p.m.
Subject: Love

Dear Precious Loved One,

Exactly! Everyone is a work in progress. No one understands that better than I. I want to be very clear—I love you and want you for who you are today, this very minute. I don't concern Myself with who you were yesterday and I don't sit in anticipation of who you'll be tomorrow. I love you right now, exactly as you are.

I don't ever look at anybody with the discerning eyes of a critic and I have no interest in spending My time digging around to uncover shortcomings or expose faults. I don't care about that. Plus, remember I already know all about you—inside and out—and I want you because you are you. I understand you're human and sometimes you may make mistakes or you may have some weaknesses, but that doesn't change how I feel about you.

From: Me <**me2@me.mail**>
To: God <**I.M.Yours@Love.God**>
Sent: February 27, 10:31 a.m.
Subject: Love

Dear God,

So I guess You love us both because of and, even sometimes, in spite of ourselves :-). I have a question: Does that mean that when we spend time with You, we don't need to worry about whether we're in a good mood or bad mood?

From: God <I.M.Yours@Love.God>
To: Me <me2@me.mail>
Sent: February 27, 10:33 a.m.
Subject: Love

Dear Precious Loved One,
Don't ever worry about that. I want to spend time with you whether you're feeling happy, hopeful, buoyant, and joyful, or needy, broken, wounded, and defeated. I'm always delighted to hear from you and I will always greet you with loving, open arms. You're Mine; I love you. I always have and I always will.
If there's one thing I want you to remember it's that I am madly in love with you and there's nothing you can do to change that. I feel this way about everyone.

From: Me <me2@me.mail>
To: God <I.M.Yours@Love.God>
Sent: February 27, 11:58 a.m.
Subject: Love

Dear God,
I'm really glad You said that because sometimes I feel like I try to edit what I tell You so I don't seem selfish or afraid or whatever else I think will make You think less of me.

From: God <I.M.Yours@Love.God>
To: Me <me2@me.mail>
Sent: February 27, 12:02 p.m.
Subject: Love

Dear Precious Loved One,
You don't ever need to censor what you tell Me or try to disguise what you really feel. Never, ever. Just be yourself—your true self. This is very important for our relationship.

From: Me <me2@me.mail>
To: God <I.M.Yours@Love.God>
Sent: March 1, 6:32 p.m.
Subject: Being Your True Self

Dear God,

    The other day You mentioned the importance of being "your true self." So does it bother You when, or if, someone tries to hide his or her real thoughts and feelings?

From: God <I.M.Yours@Love.God>
To: Me <me2@me.mail>
Sent: March 1, 6:35 p.m.
Subject: Being Your True Self

Dear Precious Loved One,

    I don't get angry, if that's what you mean. I do feel compassion for people in these situations because it's usually when they don't feel good about themselves, for whatever reason. That's when they need Me the most. So I can help them feel better and get closer to returning to their best selves. Plus, I feel sorry because it really is a waste of time since I know all about them already and see right through attempts at disguising their thoughts and feelings.

From: Me <me2@me.mail>
To: God <I.M.Yours@Love.God>
Sent: March 1, 7:01 p.m.
Subject: Being Your True Self

Dear God,

    So how do we stop doing that?

From: God <I.M.Yours@Love.God>
To: Me <me2@me.mail>
Sent: March 1, 7:04 p.m.
Subject: Being Your True Self

Dear Precious Loved One,
As with so many things in a relationship with Me, it comes down to trust. Just trust that I will continue to love you regardless of anything you say, do, or feel.
Let Me tell you, it gives Me great joy when someone realizes he or she can't hide anything from Me, and*, more importantly, there's no need to. I've said it a million times: I love you just as you are. It doesn't matter if you're being your best self or your worst self; My love for you is constant. Understanding this, and embracing it, can be a real break-through for some people.*

From: Me <me2@me.mail>
To: God <I.M.Yours@Love.God>
Sent: March 2, 7:49 a.m.
Subject: Being Your True Self

Dear God,
What do You mean by breakthrough? (You mentioned this last night.)

From: God <I.M.Yours@Love.God>
To: Me <me2@me.mail>
Sent: March 2, 7:52 a.m.
Subject: Being Your True Self

Dear Precious Loved One,
When someone becomes aware that My love truly comes with no boundaries or conditions, it can—and often does—change the depth and

breadth of our relationship. Instead of coming to Me with trepidation, he or she comes to Me with trust. Instead of coming to Me closed, he or she comes to Me open.

The more trusting and open someone is, the more fully he or she can experience the totality of My love. And once someone feels and knows the depth of My love, he or she can become a vessel of joy—for him or herself and for others.

From: Me **<me2@me.mail>**
To: God **<I.M.Yours@Love.God>**
Sent: March 5, 8:21 p.m.
Subject: Being CEO

Dear God,

Once in a homily about the parable of the woman and the lost coin, I heard a priest note that, given the historical context, the woman's use of oil to light her lamp to find just one coin would not have been considered very cost-effective, since oil was so expensive and she still had nine other coins. He went on to suggest that, similarly, Your love might not always be considered "cost-effective" by some standards because You spend a lot of love on the one individual who is lost, even though there are so many others who are not lost.

I started thinking about how corporations and all kinds of businesses constantly strive to be as cost-effective as possible. I laughed a little envisioning You as a CEO, like the CEO of the universe, and how You would be the opposite of most, if not all, other CEOs.

From: God <I.M.Yours@Love.God>
To: Me <me2@me.mail>
Sent: March 5, 8:24 p.m.
Subject: Being CEO

Dear Precious Loved One,

Yes, I imagine My way is very different. My goals are not money driven—they are rooted in joy, peace, love, and happiness. My bottom line has nothing to do with profits or earnings. My bottom line and success are measured by the amount of joy, peace, love, and happiness that permeates your life.

From: Me <me2@me.mail>
To: God <I.M.Yours@Love.God>
Sent: March 7, 9:13 a.m.
Subject: Being CEO

Dear God,

As the CEO of the universe, I also can't imagine You rating and rewarding people based on how they've performed.

From: God <I.M.Yours@Love.God>
To: Me <me2@me.mail>
Sent: March 7, 9:16 a.m.
Subject: Being CEO

Dear Precious Loved One,

With Me, there is no such thing as a meritocracy. In fact, a relationship with Me is about as far from a meritocracy as you can get. Everyone receives the same amount of love—100% for everyone all the time. This is never based on merit and never will be. I don't love people because of anything they've done, achieved, or acquired. No one gets "promoted" for

doing good deeds. No one is singled out for a reward; everyone is special.
You are each special to Me.

From: Me <me2@me.mail>
To: God <I.M.Yours@Love.God>
Sent: March 7, 2:22 p.m.
Subject: Being CEO

Dear God,
     And I'm sure You don't fire anyone or turn people away for not doing a good job.

From: God <I.M.Yours@Love.God>
To: Me <me2@me.mail>
Sent: March 7, 2:25 p.m.
Subject: Being CEO

Dear Precious Loved One,
     I am always inclusive; there's no need to turn anyone away, ever.

From: Me <me2@me.mail>
To: God <I.M.Yours@Love.God>
Sent: March 8, 7:46 a.m.
Subject: Being CEO

Dear God,
     What about when someone wants to leave You voluntarily? Like when people prepare to leave a job. When they give notice, the employer may or may not try to get those people to stay. In the end, if they don't get their way, the employers sometimes end up saying "good riddance; we didn't want them anyway."

From: God <I.M.Yours@Love.God>
To: Me <me2@me.mail>
Sent: March 8, 7:51 a.m.
Subject: Being CEO

Dear Precious Loved One,
Well with Me, it's quite the opposite. I don't want anyone to leave, ever. But I never get angry if you leave and I don't ever hold a grudge. I always want you, and anyone else, to come back to Me. And I always welcome you back with great joy.
Even when you've stepped away from Me, My love never stops. I always yearn for the day you return. My heart aches if you (or someone else) leave. I can never replace you. You are special and I love you no matter what. I don't love you because of past accomplishments or based on future potential. It's never "what have you done for me lately." I love you for who you are right now.

From: Me <me2@me.mail>
To: God <I.M.Yours@Love.God>
Sent: March 8, 8:15 a.m.
Subject: Being CEO

Dear God,
When You say these things, it all sounds so very different from the way things often are in the work world.

From: God <I.M.Yours@Love.God>
To: Me <me2@me.mail>
Sent: March 8, 8:19 a.m.
Subject: Being CEO

Dear Precious Loved One,
There is one big difference that sets the tone for everything. I've heard people say, "It's not personal; it's business." (And from what I've

seen, this is often spoken when they've made a decision that will enhance their bottom line, and they have hurt someone else in the process.)

I do things the other way. With Me it's always personal; it's never business. You are a cherished child of God. That is personal to Me. Everything I do is based on My love for you and it is 100% personal. Everything I do is related to your well-being and how I can help you be happy and filled with peace and joy.

Tuesday, March 10, 8:21 a.m.

I was just laughing to myself, wondering if You had a résumé what would be on it?

8:23 a.m.

I don't usually get asked about a résumé :-). But it might be a good way to let people know all the ways they can experience My love.

8:24 a.m.

> *I will send you one so you can get an idea of what it would be like.*

8:26 a.m.

> That would be great. Thanks!

From: God <**I.M.Yours@Love.God**>
To: Me <**me2@me.mail**>
Sent: March 11, 7:43 a.m.
Subject: Résumé

Dear Precious Loved One,
I attached a copy of My résumé. I hope it's helpful. I'm here if you have any questions.

God's Résumé

Unlimited capacity and ability to take on a variety of roles in response to your changing needs. Available day or night.

Vast experience, including but not limited to:

Healer: I help to transform physical and emotional wounds so they lose their sting and no longer hurt you. Sharing your pain with Me can heal your deepest wounds.

Friend/Companion: The antithesis of a fair-weather friend, I am your constant companion through good times and bad. When the going gets tough, you can be certain that I am walking with you and holding your hand. You are never alone when you invite Me into your life.

Consoler: I am always here to help you through your disappointments, large or small. You invariably find solace when you share your sorrows with Me.

Comforter: I am available whenever you need a shoulder to cry on. Without exception, I am here to pick up the pieces when it seems like your world is falling apart.

Supporter: I give you the encouragement you need to take the next step when you're afraid. I am a perpetual source of reassurance when you are plagued by uncertainty.

Listener: I am all ears whenever you want to talk about what's on your mind and in your heart. An attentive listener, I am never preoccupied and am always interested in what you have to say.

Cheerleader: No one delights in your successes more than I do. I am always ready to cheer you on, share in your joy and revel in your triumphs.

Adviser: I am your most trusted adviser. I never fail to answer your requests for advice and My counsel is always in your best interest.

Confidant: Whatever you share with Me is between us only. You have the freedom to expose your most intimate secrets to Me and never feel you need to conceal your real feelings. Nothing is off limits. You can always be your true self with Me.

Teacher: I want to help you learn and grow. I always guide you to the path that leads to a place where you will thrive.

From: Me <me2@me.mail>
To: God <I.M.Yours@Love.God>
Sent: March 11, 8:46 a.m.
Subject: Résumé

Dear God,
     Wow! That's quite a résumé. I guess I never really thought of You in all those ways.

From: God <I.M.Yours@Love.God>
To: Me <me2@me.mail>
Sent: March 11, 8:48 a.m.
Subject: Résumé

Dear Precious Loved One,
     These are just some of the ways you, and others, can encounter My love. I can come to My loved ones in any capacity they need.

From: Me <me2@me.mail>
To: God <I.M.Yours@Love.God>
Sent: March 12, 12:06 p.m.
Subject: Résumé

Dear God,
　　Do You think people realize all that You can do? I don't think I did.

From: God <I.M.Yours@Love.God>
To: Me <me2@me.mail>
Sent: March 12, 12:08 p.m.
Subject: Résumé

Dear Precious Loved One,
　　I think some do and others may not. For example, if someone's interaction with Me is strictly on Sunday, he or she may not have had a chance to encounter Me in some of the ways I described in My résumé.

From: Me <me2@me.mail>
To: God <I.M.Yours@Love.God>
Sent: March 12, 5:45 p.m.
Subject: Résumé

Dear God,
　　What would You want to tell those people, or anyone really?

From: God <I.M.Yours@Love.God>
To: Me <me2@me.mail>
Sent: March 12, 5:47 p.m.
Subject: Résumé

Dear Precious Loved One,
I would want them to know that, although I am very singular in My love for them, I am not one-dimensional. I would also encourage them to broaden their interaction with Me so they can see that and they can encounter My love in new and different ways. I have so much to share and they won't really get a chance to experience first-hand all that I have to offer if their time with Me is limited to Sundays, for example. In short, I would say: I'm not one-dimensional so why let your interaction with Me be one-dimensional?

From: Me <me2@me.mail>
To: God <I.M.Yours@Love.God>
Sent: March 14, 8:11 a.m.
Subject: Résumé

Dear God,
Do You get annoyed when we limit how and when we spend time with You?

From: God <I.M.Yours@Love.God>
To: Me <me2@me.mail>
Sent: March 14, 8:12 a.m.
Subject: Résumé

Dear Precious Loved One,
No, I don't get annoyed. I understand that people may be comfortable and content with having time set aside for Me on Sundays. But I

also know that with a deeper and more active relationship with Me, they could be experiencing so much more.

It would be like having a smartphone and only making phone calls with it. Yes, of course, phones are for calling people. But with a smartphone, you can do so much more—search the web, text, listen to music, download apps, take photos, and much more. So why limit your experience by restricting yourself to just phone calls?

I want to encourage people to engage with Me more fully and explore the depth of My love. I just want people to know that the more we interact, the richer and more rewarding our relationship will be. For Me, it comes down to this: The more ways I get to show you how much I love you, the better.

From: Me <me2@me.mail>
To: God <I.M.Yours@Love.God>
Sent: March 16, 7:27 p.m.
Subject: Résumé

Dear God,
From what You're saying and what I see on Your résumé, it seems like You have something for everyone. You're a little like "one-stop shopping."

From: God <I.M.Yours@Love.God>
To: Me <me2@me.mail>
Sent: March 16, 7:29 p.m.
Subject: Résumé

Dear Precious Loved One,
You could say that. All people can come to Me and I can help them, regardless of who is asking and what they need.

Here's a way of thinking about it: When you look at a shopping mall, it's a collection of stores intended to provide for people's needs all in

one place. Not every store is the same because shoppers go there for differ-
ent reasons. Their experiences in the mall will vary depending on their
individual situations, e.g., what they're looking for, how long they stay.

Well you can think of Me as a mall, but instead of stores with all
different merchandise, My mall is filled with love. I don't offer a shopping
experience. Instead, in My mall, let's call it the Mall of Love, people get
to experience My love and encounter Me in different ways depending on
what they need at any given time. And just so you know, the Mall of Love
is open 24/7 and everything is custom-made.

Your experience will be different from someone else's, and may vary
from day to day, or even hour to hour. With each encounter, i.e., visit to
the mall, I respond to your changing needs and reveal My love for you in
the way you need it at that moment.

From: Me <me2@me.mail>
To: God <I.M.Yours@Love.God>
Sent: March 16, 7:45 p.m.
Subject: Résumé

Dear God,
Can You give me an example of what You mean?

From: God <I.M.Yours@Love.God>
To: Me <me2@me.mail>
Sent: March 16, 7:46 p.m.
Subject: Résumé

Dear Precious Loved One,
Well, if you're having "one of those days" (or weeks !) when you feel
like everything is going wrong, come to Me, a.k.a. the Mall of Love, and
you can cry on My shoulder and experience Me as the One Who Comforts
and helps you through the rough patches. At another time, maybe you
just want someone to talk to. On those days, you can tell Me all about

what's on your mind and what you're feeling, and experience Me as the One Who Listens. You can always pour out your heart to Me. Others may come to Me after suffering a terrible disappointment or to share their sorrows. They will experience Me as the One Who Consoles and offers solace to them.

So you see, while I might provide one-stop shopping, My response to My loved ones' needs is never "one size fits all." Every encounter with Me is tailor-made and designed especially for that person at that moment in his or her life.

So the next time you need something, anything, just come to the Mall of Love and spend some time with Me. I have exactly what you need.

Sunday, March 18, 8:32 a.m.

Can we talk more about trust?

8:33 a.m.

It seems like it is at the center of a relationship with You.

8:35 a.m.

Trust is crucial to any relationship.

8:37 a.m.

So if You had one piece of relationship advice, what would it be?

8:38 a.m.

The more trust and the less ego you bring with you, the better.

From: Me **<me2@me.mail>**
To: God **<I.M.Yours@Love.God>**
Sent: March 19, 12:04 p.m.
Subject: Trust and Ego

Dear God,
    Do You think that our egos get in the way of having a closer relationship with You?

From: God **<I.M.Yours@Love.God>**
To: Me **<me2@me.mail>**
Sent: March 19, 12:06 p.m.
Subject: Trust and Ego

Dear Precious Loved One,
    Egos can get in the way, mostly because they often come with the need to control things.

And if you're spending your time and energy trying to control your world—whether it's at home, at work, or in your relationships—you're discounting the role that I have in your life. When your ego is running the show, you're not relying on Me and may be pushing Me to the background. I've heard some people even define ego as Edging God Out.

From: Me **<me2@me.mail>**
To: God **<I.M.Yours@Love.God>**
Sent: March 19, 1:37 p.m.
Subject: Trust and Ego

Dear God,
It sounds like ego and trust don't go well together.

From: God **<I.M.Yours@Love.God>**
To: Me **<me2@me.mail>**
Sent: March 19, 1:38 p.m.
Subject: Trust and Ego

Dear Precious Loved One,
Usually not. With one, you're trying to be "big" and in charge; with the other, you're being "small" and giving up control.
Remember, My ways are not the ways of the world. In the world, bigger is perceived as better, but with Me, smaller is better.

From: Me **<me2@me.mail>**
To: God **<I.M.Yours@Love.God>**
Sent: March 20, 7:48 a.m.
Subject: Trust and Ego

Dear God,
What do You mean by "small?"

From: God <I.M.Yours@Love.God>
To: Me <me2@me.mail>
Sent: March 20, 7:50 a.m.
Subject: Trust and Ego

Dear Precious Loved One,
When I say small, I don't mean unimportant or insignificant. I mean that you're putting Me first and placing your trust in Me. When you embrace your "smallness," you put your life in My hands and say yes to My plan for you.

From: Me <me2@me.mail>
To: God <I.M.Yours@Love.God>
Sent: March 22, 8:02 a.m.
Subject: Trust and Ego

Dear God,
So it sounds like the more we trust, the smaller we become. And as we allow ourselves to become smaller, we let You be in charge and our ego stops running the show. That actually seems pretty straightforward.

From: God <I.M.Yours@Love.God>
To: Me <me2@me.mail>
Sent: March 22, 8:04 a.m.
Subject: Trust and Ego

Dear Precious Loved One,
It's not complicated. Things with Me are never complicated. But for some people, it's not always easy.

From: Me <me2@me.mail>
To: God <I.M.Yours@Love.God>
Sent: March 22, 8:06 a.m.
Subject: Trust and Ego

Dear God,
> Do You think it's just human nature?

From: God <I.M.Yours@Love.God>
To: Me <me2@me.mail>
Sent: March 22, 8:09 a.m.
Subject: Trust and Ego

Dear Precious Loved One,
> *That depends on the human :-). In general, I think the stronger the ego, the more difficult it can be.*
> *Some people stay close to Me at all times and look to Me for guidance continuously. For others, it can be a struggle with every little thing. And then there are those whose life experience includes times of real closeness to Me, along with times when their egos dominate and they drift away or resist My ways.*

From: Me <me2@me.mail>
To: God <I.M.Yours@Love.God>
Sent: March 22, 8:59 a.m.
Subject: Ego and Forgiveness

Dear God,
> Is that what happens when we don't want to forgive someone? In our hearts we know You want us to forgive, but our heads say no.

From: God <I.M.Yours@Love.God>
To: Me <me2@me.mail>
Sent: March 22, 9:02 a.m.
Subject: Ego and Forgiveness

Dear Precious Loved One,
Yes. Forgiveness is one of those things that the ego doesn't really understand and often resists.
When you're having trouble forgiving someone who has hurt you, that little voice telling you that forgiving makes that other person right and you wrong is your ego. Or that voice may tell you that forgiving is "giving in," or that you are betraying yourself. In short, the ego will try to convince you that forgiving is a sign of weakness and diminishes you in some way.

From: Me <me2@me.mail>
To: God <I.M.Yours@Love.God>
Sent: March 22, 11:49 a.m.
Subject: Ego and Forgiveness

Dear God,
Is that ever true?

From: God <I.M.Yours@Love.God>
To: Me <me2@me.mail>
Sent: March 22, 11:52 a.m.
Subject: Ego and Forgiveness

Dear Precious Loved One,
Never. Nothing could be further from the truth. Forgiveness does not diminish you, ever. In fact, forgiveness is what helps make you whole after you have suffered a hurt.

It is the beautiful act of opening your heart to forgiveness that mends you and ultimately enhances your capacity to give and receive love.

From: Me **<me2@me.mail>**
To: God **<I.M.Yours@Love.God>**
Sent: March 24, 7:51 a.m.
Subject: Ego and Forgiveness

Dear God,
I've been thinking a lot about what You said about forgiveness. In a way, it sounds like it's when we *don't* forgive that we diminish ourselves.

From: God **<I.M.Yours@Love.God>**
To: Me **<me2@me.mail>**
Sent: March 24, 7:53 a.m.
Subject: Ego and Forgiveness

Dear Precious Loved One,
When you decide not to forgive and instead choose to hold on to anger and resentment, you certainly limit the room in your heart for love and joy.

From: Me **<me2@me.mail>**
To: God **<I.M.Yours@Love.God>**
Sent: March 24, 8:39 a.m.
Subject: Ego and Forgiveness

Dear God,
So it seems like the ego tries to make the act of forgiveness into something that it isn't, i.e., right vs. wrong, win vs. lose, and equates being wrong and losing with forgiveness.
But what about when we ask *You* for forgiveness?

From: God <**I.M.Yours@Love.God**>
To: Me <**me2@me.mail**>
Sent: March 24, 8:42 a.m.
Subject: Ego and Forgiveness

Dear Precious Loved One,
   That can be problematic for the ego too, but for different reasons.

From: Me <**me2@me.mail**>
To: God <**I.M.Yours@Love.God**>
Sent: March 24, 3:21 p.m.
Subject: Ego and Forgiveness

Dear God,
   Why? What do You mean?

From: God <**I.M.Yours@Love.God**>
To: Me <**me2@me.mail**>
Sent: March 24, 3:24 p.m.
Subject: Ego and Forgiveness

Dear Precious Loved One,
   Remember, My ways are not the ways of the world. With Me, there is no quid pro quo, no garnering favor or earning things like forgiveness. Whatever I give you—whether it's My forgiveness, My Grace, or anything else—is a gift. I give it to you without reservation. It's free; it can never be earned. I give it to you purely out of love.
   This doesn't make sense to the ego that thrives in a world in which people constantly work, or even struggle, to get what they think they deserve. There is nothing you can do to persuade Me to forgive you or enhance the way I feel about you.
   With Me, forgiveness is always possible, and My love for you is constant. This is who I am; I don't change based on what you've done

or what you have. You get all of Me all the time, just because you are you and I love you. This, of course, is troublesome for the ego because it goes against the ego's need for earning, deserving, winning, and judging.

From: Me **<me2@me.mail>**
To: God **<I.M.Yours@Love.God>**
Sent: March 24, 7:41 p.m.
Subject: Ego and Forgiveness

Dear God,

So when that little voice in our heads tells us what we've done is unforgivable, or that we're not lovable, it's just our egos?

From: God **<I.M.Yours@Love.God>**
To: Me **<me2@me.mail>**
Sent: March 24, 7:44 p.m.
Subject: Ego and Forgiveness

Dear Precious Loved One,

It's the ego's way of keeping you from the security of My embrace and from reveling in the joy of My unconditional love. (This may be why some people equate ego with edging God out.)

Let Me put it another way so you can really see the difference between My way and the way of the ego:

A relationship with Me is not like spending time in a classroom or place of work, which are often structured around a set of standards that measure achievement and reward (or maybe penalize) people based on performance.

Instead, a relationship with Me is like standing under a waterfall where there is a constant flow of love from Me, love that refreshes your soul. I shower you with My love unceasingly. You can't stop it; you can't earn it. It just is.

Throughout your life, you're drenched in My love regardless of anything you do, acquire, or achieve. This, of course, invalidates everything the ego thrives upon. The ego wants you to see My love as a faucet that goes on and off in response to your behavior. But it can never, and will never, be that way. My love is constantly flowing to you.

From: Me **<me2@me.mail>**
To: God **<I.M.Yours@Love.God>**
Sent: March 27, 8:02 p.m.
Subject: Our Egos

Dear God,
　　We don't start out with our egos so much in charge, do we? So how do we get that way?

From: God **<I.M.Yours@Love.God>**
To: Me **<me2@me.mail>**
Sent: March 27, 8:05 p.m.
Subject: Our Egos

Dear Precious Loved One,
　　Many people are taught, from when they're very young, to be self-sufficient and independent. They want to control their destiny and not rely on anyone or anything. If you're raised this way and equate control with success, then giving up control by trusting Me may seem like failure.
　　So for some people, trusting Me goes against everything they've learned. When I see how hard people work at establishing and maintaining their authority and power, it's not surprising that trusting Me and losing control seems frightening.

From: Me <me2@me.mail>
To: God <I.M.Yours@Love.God>
Sent: March 28, 4:06 p.m.
Subject: Our Egos

Dear God,

How do we trust You more and abandon our need for "bigness?" How do we do it, if it goes against what we've been taught and how we live our day-to-day lives?

From: God <I.M.Yours@Love.God>
To: Me <me2@me.mail>
Sent: March 28, 4:09 p.m.
Subject: Our Egos

Dear Precious Loved One,

Like so many other things, it takes practice. Trusting Me more simply boils down to saying no to the ego and giving up the desire to be in charge all the time.

From: Me <me2@me.mail>
To: God <I.M.Yours@Love.God>
Sent: March 30, 9:06 a.m.
Subject: Our Egos

Dear God,

It sounds like we need to let go of some old, ingrained habits and practice some new ones. I guess what we really have to do is stop edging God out by ignoring the demands of the ego and start edging God in by trusting You more and more.

From: God <**I.M.Yours@Love.God**>
To: Me <**me2@me.mail**>
Sent: March 30, 9:09 a.m.
Subject: Our Egos

Dear Precious Loved One,

To some people, this may be a fundamental shift in their way of thinking and being. I realize that discarding or changing old habits isn't necessarily easy, so I will always be there to help. All you need to do is try.

Remember, anytime you're trying to get closer to Me, I give you all the help and Grace you need; I never refuse you.

From: Me <**me2@me.mail**>
To: God <**I.M.Yours@Love.God**>
Sent: April 1, 12:08 p.m.
Subject: Our Egos

Dear God,

What happens if we try to trust You, but our ego wins out and we end up going back to wanting and struggling to be in charge?

From: God <**I.M.Yours@Love.God**>
To: Me <**me2@me.mail**>
Sent: April 1, 12:10 p.m.
Subject: Our Egos

Dear Precious Loved One,

Just try again. Your journey may have ups and downs. You might feel like you take two steps forward and one step back. That's okay. Don't worry, just keep trying. The more you try, and the more you devote your energy to trusting Me, the more you will notice My presence in your life.

From: Me <me2@me.mail>
To: God <I.M.Yours@Love.God>
Sent: April 1, 7:58 p.m.
Subject: Your Presence

Dear God,
    Is that what You want for all of us—to feel Your presence in our lives?

From: God <I.M.Yours@Love.God>
To: Me <me2@me.mail>
Sent: April 1, 8:02 p.m.
Subject: Your Presence

Dear Precious Loved One,
    Yes, I want you, and all My loved ones, to continually feel the safety of My embrace and experience the enormity of My love and the joy of being taken care of in the deepest and most profound way.

From: God <I.M.Yours@Love.God>
To: Me <me2@me.mail>
Sent: April 2, 9:16 p.m.
Subject: Something Else

Dear Precious Loved One,
    There is something else that I really desire for you and all My loved ones. I want you to be so confident in My love for you and feel such a close communion with Me that you think of your life as a love story. A love story about you and Me, and between you and Me. One where we go through the days together and where I help you create and experience the story of your life.

I don't want you to think I'm just with you for the big occasions like births, deaths, weddings etc., and that I'm sitting on the sidelines or staying in the background for the rest.

I am sharing every moment with you, and walking with you 24/7, trudging with you when the path seems arduous and helping you with the uphill struggles; stepping lightheartedly when the path is saturated in sunlight and joy; and meandering along and keeping you company when things seem mundane and quiet.

From: Me <me2@me.mail>
To: God <I.M.Yours@Love.God>
Sent: April 3, 7:29 a.m.
Subject: Love Story

Dear God,
     When You talk about a "love story" it sounds like what's in the movies and books, and a lot more personal than what I am used to thinking about with God.

From: God <I.M.Yours@Love.God>
To: Me <me2@me.mail>
Sent: April 3, 7:31 a.m.
Subject: Love Story

Dear Precious Loved One,
     What are you used to?

From: Me <me2@me.mail>
To: God <I.M.Yours@Love.God>
Sent: April 3, 3:02 p.m.
Subject: Love Story

Dear God,

Don't get the wrong idea. Love is definitely part of what I associate with You and religion. Of course, in church, it's not unusual to hear about loving your neighbor, about Your love for us. And we're probably all familiar with the commandment "Love God with all your heart," but I don't think about any of this in terms of a love story.

From: God <I.M.Yours@Love.God>
To: Me <me2@me.mail>
Sent: April 3, 3:06 p.m.
Subject: Love Story

Dear Precious Loved One,
*   And when you hear "Love God with all your heart," what comes to mind?*

From: Me <me2@me.mail>
To: God <I.M.Yours@Love.God>
Sent: April 3, 4:45 p.m.
Subject: Love Story

Dear God,

Since it's a commandment, I know it's important and is something that I try very hard to do. But in the end, it's probably more of a far-off, unattainable ideal rather than a real-life experience that relates to a personal relationship with You.

From: God <I.M.Yours@Love.God>
To: Me <me2@me.mail>
Sent: April 3, 4:48 p.m.
Subject: Love Story

Dear Precious Loved One,
Have you ever heard anything that makes you think about a personal relationship with Me?

From: Me <me2@me.mail>
To: God <I.M.Yours@Love.God>
Sent: April 3, 7:21 p.m.
Subject: Love Story

Dear God,
Well, once or twice I've heard a priest mention "falling in love with God," but I don't really count that.

From: God <I.M.Yours@Love.God>
To: Me <me2@me.mail>
Sent: April 3, 7:24 p.m.
Subject: Love Story

Dear Precious Loved One,
Why?

From: Me <me2@me.mail>
To: God <I.M.Yours@Love.God>
Sent: April 3, 7:58 p.m.
Subject: Love Story

Dear God,

Because I assumed he was just talking about his own life, i.e., he fell in love with You and that's why he became a priest. And that's what happens for nuns and other religious. He wasn't talking about regular people like me.

To tell You the truth, I couldn't really understand why he said it. They seemed like words that don't really belong together in the same sentence, and didn't make sense for just about everyone there. Then I figured maybe he was just trying to shock us or get our attention.

From: God <I.M.Yours@Love.God>
To: Me <me2@me.mail>
Sent: April 3, 8:02 p.m.
Subject: Love Story

Dear Precious Loved One,

Well, it sounds like he did get your attention. By using the familiar phrase "falling in love" and adding "with God," he was shining a light on something you, or others, may not have considered before.

It was an invitation to explore the depth and breadth of the relationship you can have with Me. He was letting you know that, contrary to what you and others may have thought, falling in love with God can and does relate to your life. It's available to everyone.

From: Me **<me2@me.mail>**
To: God **<I.M.Yours@Love.God>**
Sent: April 5, 5:10 p.m.
Subject: Love Story

Dear God,

I guess we need to somehow move from thinking of "love God with all your heart" as just an impersonal commandment, or maybe even an abstract concept, to participating in an animated, emotional relationship with You. I'm not totally sure how to do that.

Maybe it's a question of approaching it from our hearts instead of our heads and replacing thinking with feeling, or maybe we need to switch from viewing the relationship as a passive one to a more active one.

From: God **<I.M.Yours@Love.God>**
To: Me **<me2@me.mail>**
Sent: April 5, 5:13 p.m.
Subject: Love Story

Dear Precious Loved One,

This may be a total reorientation for some people, but for others it may be only a slight shift. Either way, the path to get there is straightforward and is the same for everyone—spend time with Me and let Me in your life.

From: Me **<me2@me.mail>**
To: God **<I.M.Yours@Love.God>**
Sent: April 5, 5:42 p.m.
Subject: Love Story

Dear God,

That's it?

From: God <I.M.Yours@Love.God>
To: Me <me2@me.mail>
Sent: April 5, 5:44 p.m.
Subject: Love Story

Dear Precious Loved One,
Yes. Just share yourself with Me. Talk to Me; tell Me your innermost thoughts, from your wildest dreams to your ordinary daily ponderings. I'm all ears. There's no need to keep anything from Me.

From: Me <me2@me.mail>
To: God <I.M.Yours@Love.God>
Sent: April 7, 9:07 a.m.
Subject: Love Story

Dear God,
I don't know about anyone else, but there are definitely some things that I'm not so eager to share—like the times I've been mean or selfish or have done or said something deliberately hurtful to someone else.

From: God <I.M.Yours@Love.God>
To: Me <me2@me.mail>
Sent: April 7, 9:09 a.m.
Subject: Love Story

Dear Precious Loved One,
I realize it may seem a little uncomfortable or unsettling if you're not used to it, but give it a try.
And I'll make you a deal: Tell Me about something that you'd rather not share; it doesn't have to be the worst thing, but something that you feel is not so great. Afterwards, if you feel better and are glad you shared,

then try it again with something that you feel is even less flattering. And if you keep liking it, keep doing it and just see what happens.

Sunday, April 8, 3:04 p.m.

One thing about that deal
You proposed yesterday,
what if I don't feel better
after sharing the bad stuff?

3:05 p.m.

Well, if you feel worse, then you don't ever have to share the "bad stuff" again.

3:09 p.m.

Never?

3:11 p.m.

Never. So do we have a deal?

3:18 p.m.

> Well, I guess I
> have nothing
> to lose.

3:19 p.m.

> *With Me, you*
> *never have*
> *anything to*
> *lose :-).*

From: Me **<me2@me.mail>**
To: God **<I.M.Yours@Love.God>**
Sent: April 10, 8:27 a.m.
Subject: Sharing the Bad Stuff

Dear God,
  You seem pretty certain that I'll be glad that I shared; otherwise, I don't think You'd say I don't have to share that stuff with You again.

From: God **<I.M.Yours@Love.God>**
To: Me **<me2@me.mail>**
Sent: April 10, 8:31 a.m.
Subject: Sharing the Bad Stuff

Dear Precious Loved One,
  Yes, I am confident, very confident, in fact. I've seen this many times, with all different types of people, but it always ends up the same.

From: Me <me2@me.mail>
To: God <I.M.Yours@Love.God>
Sent: April 10, 11:43 a.m.
Subject: Sharing the Bad Stuff

Dear God,
    What happens?

From: God <I.M.Yours@Love.God>
To: Me <me2@me.mail>
Sent: April 10, 11:47 a.m.
Subject: Sharing the Bad Stuff

Dear Precious Loved One,
    As people spend time with Me and become more confident and comfortable, little by little they communicate more openly and freely. In revealing themselves to Me at a deeper level, they realize that no matter what they say and do (including what they think of as "the bad stuff"), I keep loving them.
    My love is absolute. There are no ifs, no boundaries and no rules.

From: Me <me2@me.mail>
To: God <I.M.Yours@Love.God>
Sent: April 13, 9:14 a.m.
Subject: Absolute, Unconditional Love

Dear God,
    I feel like that phrase "God's love is absolute" is one of those things we all hear but don't necessarily understand or don't get to experience what it means in an active or concrete way.

From: God <I.M.Yours@Love.God>
To: Me <me2@me.mail>
Sent: April 13, 9:16 a.m.
Subject: Absolute, Unconditional Love

Dear Precious Loved One,
That's precisely why I encourage you or anyone else to open yourself up and share your true self with Me, even if it means stepping outside your comfort zone. Remember, I don't care about your wounds, fears, missteps, or doubts, or anything that you think might make you unlovable. I always love you and want you.

From: Me <me2@me.mail>
To: God <I.M.Yours@Love.God>
Sent: April 13, 9:21 a.m.
Subject: Absolute, Unconditional Love

Dear God,
    That sounds reassuring!

From: God <I.M.Yours@Love.God>
To: Me <me2@me.mail>
Sent: April 13, 9:24 a.m.
Subject: Absolute, Unconditional Love

Dear Precious Loved One,
Come to Me just as you are, fully exposed and open to My Love. I promise you will always find Me eagerly waiting for you with outstretched arms.
The more you engage and interact with Me, the more you will experience first-hand that I am totally in love with you. You'll like it. I promise.

From: Me <me2@me.mail>
To: God <I.M.Yours@Love.God>
Sent: April 16, 12:07 p.m.
Subject: Absolute, Unconditional Love

Dear God,

The other day You mentioned that, over time, people realize that You love them all the time, no matter what. How do You know when they realize it? How can You tell?

From: God <I.M.Yours@Love.God>
To: Me <me2@me.mail>
Sent: April 16, 12:10 p.m.
Subject: Absolute, Unconditional Love

Dear Precious Love One,

Because they continue spending time with Me and allowing our connection to evolve and grow. I see the inner peace and contentment that shine through when people feel infinitely loved by Me. And as they continue to shine more brightly, then I also know that they have ultimately fallen in love with Me.

From: Me <me2@me.mail>
To: God <I.M.Yours@Love.God>
Sent: April 16, 12:16 p.m.
Subject: Aha!

Dear God,

So this is what the priest was alluding to when he said "falling in love with God"?

From: God <I.M.Yours@Love.God>
To: Me <me2@me.mail>
Sent: April 16, 12:19 p.m.
Subject: Aha!

Dear Precious Loved One,
    Yes. So I invite you to experience the vastness of My love for you.

From: Me <me2@me.mail>
To: God <I.M.Yours@Love.God>
Sent: April 16, 12:45 p.m.
Subject: Aha!

Dear God,
    And fall in love with You.

From: God <I.M.Yours@Love.God>
To: Me <me2@me.mail>
Sent: April 16, 12:49 p.m.
Subject: Aha!

Dear Precious Loved One,
    Yes :-). (By the way, I should warn you, people have told Me I'm irresistible.)
    Oh, and one more thing. I know in some relationships when people begin falling in love, they wonder and get nervous about how the other person feels; they ask themselves that scary question, "What if he/she doesn't love me back?" Well, you don't have to worry about that with Me. I loved you first and always. And like you said before, you have nothing to lose!

From: Me **<me2@me.mail>**
To: God **<I.M.Yours@Love.God>**
Sent: April 16, 1:00 p.m.
Subject: Yes

Dear God,
    I accept Your invitation :-).

From: Me **<me2@me.mail>**
To: God **<I.M.Yours@Love.God>**
Sent: April 19, 7:31 p.m.
Subject: Favorite Things

Dear God,
    If You had to make a list of the top ten things You want people to know about You, what would be on it?

From: God **<I.M.Yours@Love.God>**
To: Me **<me2@me.mail>**
Sent: April 19, 7:38 p.m.
Subject: Favorite Things

Dear Precious Loved One,
    How about I make it God's Top Eleven List, to avoid confusion with the Ten Commandments?
    Here goes, and these are in no special order:

1. I am here for you 24/7. *You have unlimited access to Me; My door is always open. You have an open invitation to spend time with Me, anytime, anywhere. And no RSVP is required.*
2. Now's the time. *Don't put off spending time with Me and getting to know Me until someday when the kids are older, when*

you retire, when you don't have to take care of your parents. Our relationship is for right now.

3. With Me it's *not* all or nothing. *If you can only spend a few minutes with Me, that's fine. Let's do that. I will never turn you away and say "Well, if it's only a few minutes then forget it." I will meet you where you are. I always love to hear from you.*

4. My love is unconditional. *You don't have to, and can't, earn it. You get 100% of My love all the time. I'll never stop loving you. Never, ever. I am completely irrational when it comes to My love for you. I can't help it :-).*

5. I'm all ears. *You can tell Me anything and I mean absolutely anything. I never get bored and I'm really, really nosy. I like to know it all, so feel free to share away.*

6. When you ask for My help, I always answer your call. *Although My timetable may not always be the same as yours, try to be patient and trust that I will deliver what's best for you at exactly the right moment. Important: When you hand over something to Me, leave it with Me.* No backsies!

7. Your joy is My priority. *I will always help you find the path that leads to joy, peace, and contentment. Think of Me as your joy compass.*

8. If you love Me (or even just like Me), tell someone. *Introduce Me to your friends or family who don't know Me. There's no such thing as too many Precious Loved Ones. With Me, it's always the more the merrier.*

9. You are very special to Me. *There is no one else like you and I love you just as you are.*

10. I love a trier. *All I ask is that you try. You don't have to be perfect.*

11. I love it when you say thank you. *My heart leaps with joy when you thank Me.*

From: Me <me2@me.mail>
To: God <I.M.Yours@Love.God>
Sent: April 21, 11:29 a.m.
Subject: Favorite Things

Dear God,
Thanks for Your Top Eleven List. I may even put that on my refrigerator. Is there anything else You want to share?

From: God <I.M.Yours@Love.God>
To: Me <me2@me.mail>
Sent: April 21, 11:33 a.m.
Subject: Favorite Things

Dear Precious Loved One,
I do have one more list of sorts. Here are some of the things I hear and the good news I'd like to share to dispel these misconceptions:

Misconception:
Having a relationship with God is reserved for priests, nuns, and others that have a religious calling.

Good news:
Getting to know Me and having an intimate, loving relationship with Me is for everyone. You don't need any special religious pedigree. You don't need any credentials at all. You just need to be. Be present, be engaged, be open, be yourself.

Misconception:

God's too busy. I shouldn't bother God unless it's an emergency or some sort of crisis.

Good news:

I am never too busy and you are never ever bothering Me. Yes, of course, come to Me if there's an emergency. But I love to hear from you on the ordinary days too, or when you need help figuring something out, or if you just want to talk. There's no bad time to visit with Me. Every "date" we have is special to Me.

Misconception:

God only really loves me and answers my prayers when I'm being good, kind, and loving; not when I've messed up.

Good news:

I don't keep track of your good deeds and mistakes so I can decide if I want to answer your prayers. I will always respond to your prayers, but never as judge, adversary, or critic. You'll receive My love and compassion in all situations (especially when you've messed up! That's often when you need it most!!).

Misconception:

Grace is only for saints, priests, nuns, other religious, and people who are really holy.

Good news:

Nope, not even close. Grace is available to everyone, and not just on special occasions.

Misconception:
I need to be at mass or at least in a church to visit with God.

Good news:
I am not a God of location. You can be with Me anytime and anywhere you choose.

Misconception:
I should stay away and keep my distance when I'm angry at God, like when I feel as if He's not answering my prayers.

Good news:
I don't ever want there to be distance between us, especially if you're angry. Don't stay away; come to Me and tell Me why you're upset. It's okay if you're angry at Me; you won't be the first. People have yelled at Me before, people who truly love Me. So don't worry, I can take it. I want to hear from you so I can ease your pain and help you feel better.

Misconception:
God's going to stop listening if I complain too much.

Good news:
I have an infinite capacity for listening to My loved ones and it's not affected by what you're sharing with Me. It doesn't matter if you're sad, dejected, and vulnerable, or cheerful, jubilant, and confident, I want to hear from you. You can always share your problems and disappointments with Me. I like to know what upsets you or hurts you, so I can help you.

I know life's not always easy. I am here for you, especially when you hit a rough patch. Of course, I do like to hear about the good things also. So don't be shy about telling Me about them too. I like to smile along with you and share in your joy and happiness.

From: Me <me2@me.mail>
To: God <I.M.Yours@Love.God>
Sent: April 22, 4:04 p.m.
Subject: Thank You

Dear God,

Thank You so much for everything. Believe it or not, I think I've run out of questions, for now anyway.

From: God <I.M.Yours@Love.God>
To: Me <me2@me.mail>
Sent: April 22, 4:07 p.m.
Subject: One More Thing

Dear Precious Loved One,

You know I'm always here if you think of anything else. I do have one more thing. It's actually a request.

From: Me <me2@me.mail>
To: God <I.M.Yours@Love.God>
Sent: April 22, 4:11 p.m.
Subject: One More Thing

Dear God,

Sure. What can *I* do for *You?*

From: God <**I.M.Yours@Love.God**>
To: Me <**me2@me.mail**>
Sent: April 22, 4:14 p.m.
Subject: One More Thing

Dear Precious Loved One,
Share this. Please share it.

From: Me <**me2@me.mail**>
To: God <**I.M.Yours@Love.God**>
Sent: April 22, 4:22 p.m.
Subject: Yes!

Dear God,
I will. I promise.

About the Author

Elaine Porter lives in Larchmont, NY. She is a member of Sts. John and Paul Parish and a graduate of the parish school. Elaine also graduated from School of the Holy Child in Rye, NY and attended Iona College, where she earned a BA in English.

CPSIA information can be obtained
at www.ICGtesting.com
Printed in the USA
BVOW11s0140200118
505609BV00008B/45/P

9 781641 915908